Multi-Level Spelling

Grades 3-6

Written by Barb Scott and Joni Turville
Illustrated by S&S Learning Materials

ISBN 1-55035-609-7
Copyright 1999
Revised January 2006
All Rights Reserved * Printed in Canada

Published in the United States by:
On the Mark Press
3909 Witmer Road PMB 175
Niagara Falls, New York
14305
www.onthemarkpress.com

Published in Canada by:
S&S Learning Materials
15 Dairy Avenue
Napanee, Ontario
K7R 1M4
www.sslearning.com

Look For Other Language Units

Multi-Level Spelling

Table of Contents

Multi-Level Spelling

Objectives

1. To increase students' spelling ability at their own level.

2. To provide the ability to remediate and challenge students.

3. To expand vocabulary.

4. To teach children about phonics and word structure.

Background Information

With the huge range in student ability within any classroom these days, it is increasingly difficult to meet their diverse needs. After spending several years in a special education program where we tailored programs for individual students, we moved to a homeroom assignment. There, we realized that the needs within the "regular" classroom were just as diverse and we needed a way to be able to remediate where necessary and challenge other students who were already proficient.

As a result, we searched through many different resources and came up with our own multi-level spelling program. The words are sequenced, and alike words are grouped together for each unit. For example, we've started with short-vowel words, so the lists for short "a" contain five different lists from easiest to hardest but all contain short "a" sounds. The lesson you would teach for that week would be for one skill (example: short "a" words), but the students would work on and study words that were appropriate for their own spelling ability.

We hope that you will find this unit helpful while you teach spelling in your classroom.

Multi-Level Spelling

Teacher Input Suggestions

Where to begin?

1. It is important to first assess where your students are in their spelling skills, both formally and informally. There are several kinds of standardized testing instruments you can use. We have used the Schonell Graded Word Spelling Test, but any one will be a good starting point.

2. Do a miscue analysis. Copy a page of each student's unedited writing. Note spelling errors made, look for patterns, in particular. Calculate the percentage of words spelled correctly by counting the number of words spelled correctly and dividing the total number of words in the passage. This is especially useful for pre- and post-testing during reporting periods.

3. Make as many spelling groups as you feel are manageable and appropriate. The lists provided allow for five different levels; you need not use all of them. You can also make easier or more difficult lists by adding to those provided.

4. The lists go from one (easiest) to five (most difficult).

5. Some words on the lists are common, and this is intentional because they are commonly misspelled in children's writing.

6. Many of the words in the more difficult lists might be ones that the students don't understand. This is intentional so that if children are confident spellers, their knowledge of vocabulary can be challenged and expanded. This makes it critical to ensure that students understand the meaning of their words and develop strategies in using a dictionary so they can locate the meaning of words that they don't know.

7. The groups we make are never static for the whole year. Students' abilities and confidence levels change throughout the school year, and we adjust the groups whenever necessary. You might want to solicit parent help in this regard, having them note if the lists being studied are too hard or too easy for their child each week.

Multi-Level Spelling

Weekly Activities

A possible format for spelling each week might include the following (but structure your activities to suit your students' needs and the structure of your program):

1. Distribute lists on Mondays. You might want to include a pre-test at this point as well.

2. Read through lists for each group, discussing the meaning of the words on each list.

3. Discuss and do any teaching required involving the words from the unit. For example: If you list contains "ie" words, teach the "i before e, except after c" rule.

4. Choose from the list of "generic" spelling activities, depending on the time you have and the type of words on the lists that week.

5. The exercises may be broken up over several days during the week or done all at once.

6. Allow time to study, to help students develop some strategies for ways to study their words.

7. You might want to have the students copy their words onto a card for their desk so they can study during any free time they have that week.

8. Post-testing occurs on Fridays.

Multi-Level Spelling

Teaching Studying Strategies

1. One method of studying alone:

   a) Look at the word.
   b) Say the word out loud.
   c) Cover the word.
   d) Write the word.
   e) Check the word.

   Do these five steps until the word is spelled correctly at least two times consecutively.

2. For spelling alone, you might want to try some other strategies which are particularly effective for kinesthetic learners, such as spelling words in salt, jello powder, pudding, shaving cream, on sandpaper or with small chalk boards.

3. Students can pair up and quiz each other on their words.

4. Students also get practice writing their words during their weekly spelling activities.

Whole Class Activities

1. Introduce the lesson by having the students brainstorm words (Example: If the lesson is on short "a", start by brainstorming and charting words with short "a"). The chart generated could be posted in the room for the week (or longer, if you choose).

2. An alternative to a charted list might be to create a laminated "word wall" which could be changed each week to correspond with that week's lesson.

Multi-Level Spelling

3. Point out any interesting ways that students might remember words, such as breaking down words into segments or making note of other parts (Example: An "island" **is** land).

4. Use computers to type out their words in a list. This is good keyboarding practice , and any use of computers always seems motivating to the kids!

5. Use some computer software resources to study. Programs such as the Learning Company's "Spellbound" allow for customized lists.

Classroom Management Ideas

Testing groups of students simultaneously sounds a bit tricky but is quite easily managed.

1. We often have the students working on an activity which they can complete independently (Example: diaries or other independent writing) while each group is tested.

2. Groups can be tested at the same time by having the teacher call out a group number and the word for their list, followed by the next pack until all the groups have finished their first word. By the time you are back to the first group, they'll have had sufficient time to write their word and then you can give each group their second word.

3. Use a parent, community volunteer or older student to volunteer to test students individually or in small groups.

4. Have spelling partners or buddies and have them give tests to each other in the older grades.

Multi-Level Spelling

"Generic" Spelling Activity Ideas

Since the students are working on different lists, one way to manage this is to assign activities that can be used for every list. The following activities can be used as an activity card or as a worksheet. The activity cards or worksheets have ideas that can be used in any order.

The top half of each sheet can be used just as an activity card and can be cut away from the lower section which contains lines for student recording. Color, mount the card on a study backing and laminate. The students will record their work in a spelling workbook.

Each sheet can also be used as a reproducible worksheet. The worksheets could be stored in folders for student access.

The teacher can assign a selection of activities for the entire class, depending on the words in the lists that week, or a "Spelling Center" could be set up where students could choose a certain number of activities to complete each week.

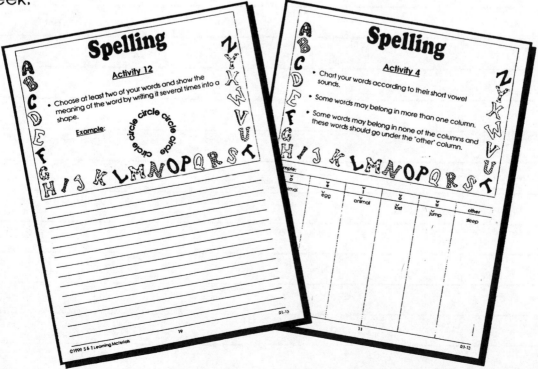

Spelling

Activity 1

Write your words in the correct **alphabetical** order.

Example: defend
degree
depart
defog

Spelling

Activity 2

Box the shape of your words.

Example: pretty

_____
_____
_____
_____
_____
_____
_____
_____
_____
_____
_____
_____
_____
_____
_____
_____

Spelling

Activity 3

- Copy your spelling words three times each. You may use printing (manuscript) or handwriting.

- Box any parts of your word that you think might be tricky to spell.

- Circle the word you wrote the neatest in each line.

1. _____ _____ _____

2. _____ _____ _____

3. _____ _____ _____

4. _____ _____ _____

5. _____ _____ _____

6. _____ _____ _____

7. _____ _____ _____

8. _____ _____ _____

9. _____ _____ _____

10. _____ _____ _____

Spelling

Activity 4

- Chart your words according to their short vowel sounds.

- Some words may belong in more than one column.

- Some words may belong in none of the columns and these words should go under the "other" column.

Example:

ă	ĕ	ĭ	ŏ	ŭ	other
ănimal	ĕgg	ănimal	lŏst	jŭmp	sleep

Spelling

Activity 5

- Chart your words according to their long vowel sounds.

- Some words may belong in more than one column.

- Some words may belong in none of the columns and these words should go under the "other" column.

Example:

$\overline{a}$	$\overline{e}$	$\overline{i}$	$\overline{o}$	$\overline{u}$	other

Spelling

Activity 6

- Clap out the "beats" or syllables for your word and tell how many syllables it has.

Example: snowman - 2 syllables

Spelling

Activity 7

- Divide your word into syllables.

Example: snow - man

_____

_____

_____

_____

_____

_____

_____

_____

_____

_____

_____

_____

_____

_____

Spelling

Activity 8

- Make rhyming words for as many words on your list as is possible. (Some words may not have another word which rhymes with it.)

Example: near - hear
shoe - true

_____

_____

_____

_____

_____

_____

_____

_____

_____

_____

_____

_____

_____

Spelling

Activity 9

- Write a synonym for as many words on your list as possible.

- You may not be able to find a synonym for every word.

- Hint: Try using a thesaurus.

Examples: little - small
mad - angry

_____
_____
_____
_____
_____
_____
_____
_____
_____
_____
_____
_____
_____

Spelling

Activity 10

- Write an opposite (antonym) for as many of your spelling words as possible.

- There may not be an antonym for all of your words.

Examples: big - little

hard - soft

Spelling

Activity 11

- Write a "Who am I?" riddle about each of your spelling words.

Example: **Riddle:** I am a word which is the opposite of dull.

Answer: sharp

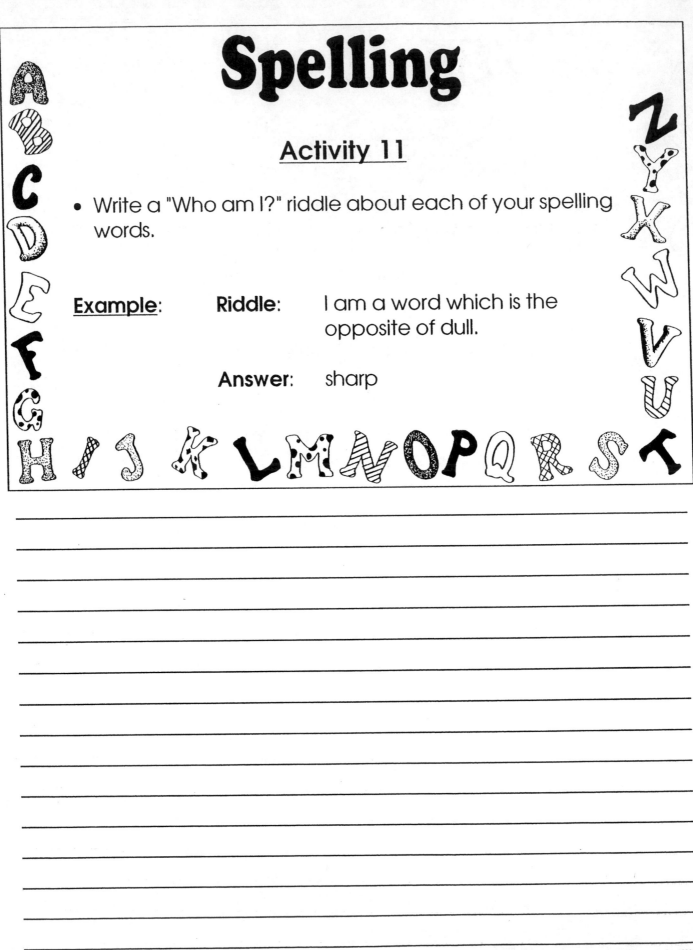

Spelling

Activity 12

- Choose at least two of your words and show the meaning of the word by writing it several times into a shape.

Example:

_____

_____

_____

_____

_____

_____

_____

_____

_____

_____

_____

_____

_____

_____

Spelling

Activity 13

- Plurals mean "more than one".

- Make as many of the words from your list into plurals.

- Use a dictionary if you're not sure how to spell the plural.

Examples: chair - chairs
leaf - leaves

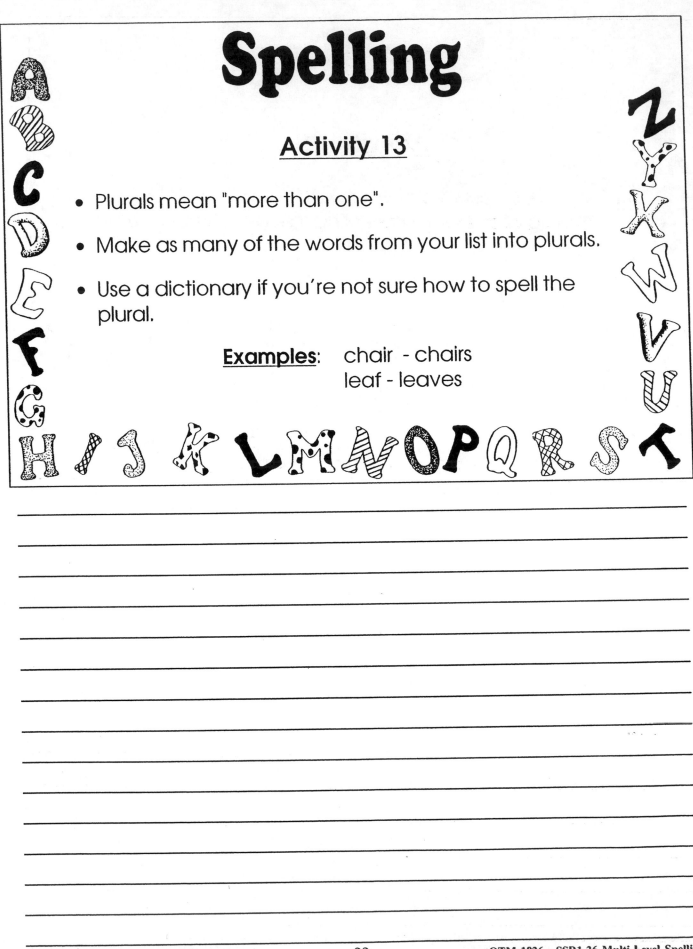

_____

_____

_____

_____

_____

_____

_____

_____

_____

_____

_____

_____

_____

_____

Spelling

Activity 14

- Look for root words and endings in your list.

- Use as many words as possible to complete the chart.

Word	Root Word	Ending
smaller	small	er
fastest	fast	est

Spelling

Activity 15

- Look up each word in the dictionary and write its meaning.

Example:

camel - an animal that lives in the desert.

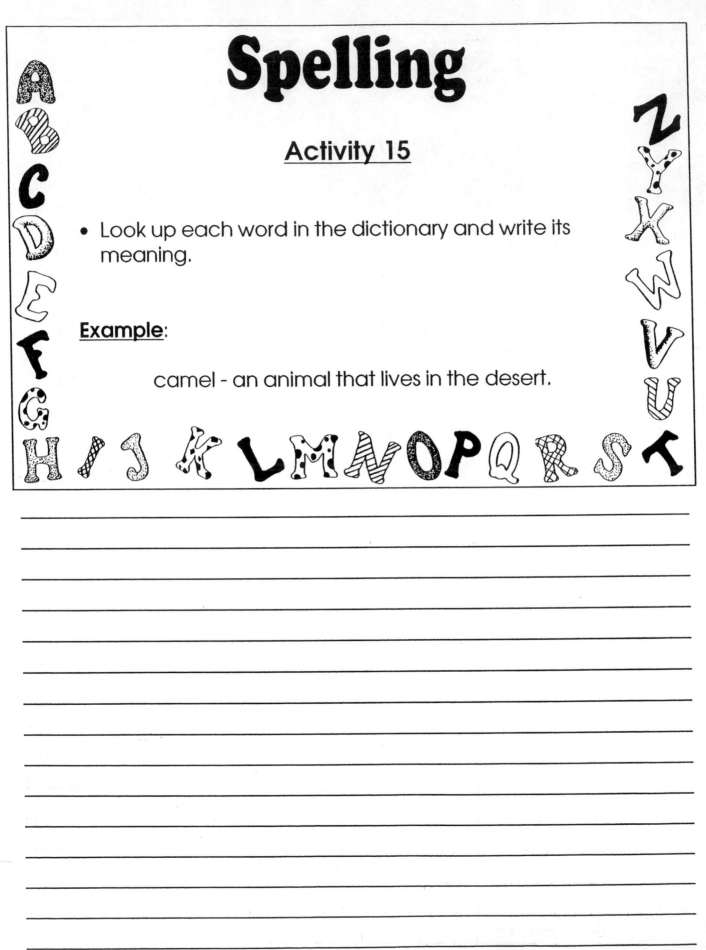

Spelling

Activity 16

- Look up each word in the dictionary and copy an example sentence.

- Hint: It is usually in italics.

Example:

cowboy - *The cowboy rounded up the cattle.*

Spelling

Activity 17

- Look up each word in the dictionary and write how it is pronounced.

Example: crystal - (kris´təl)

_____

_____

_____

_____

_____

_____

_____

_____

_____

_____

_____

_____

_____

Spelling

Activity 18

- Look up each word in the dictionary and write its part of speech such as noun, verb, adjective, adverb, conjunction, etc.

Examples: door - noun
sleep - verb
and - conjunction

Spelling

Activity 19

- Use your words and the grid below to construct a word search.

- Hint: Hide your words first, trying to overlap some of them, and then fill in the blank squares with random letters.

Spelling

Activity 20

- Write a sentence using as many of the words from your list as possible.

- Try using __all__ of them!

- Your sentence must make sense.

_____
_____
_____
_____
_____
_____
_____
_____
_____
_____
_____
_____

Spelling

Activity 21

- Write a short story using all of the words from your list.

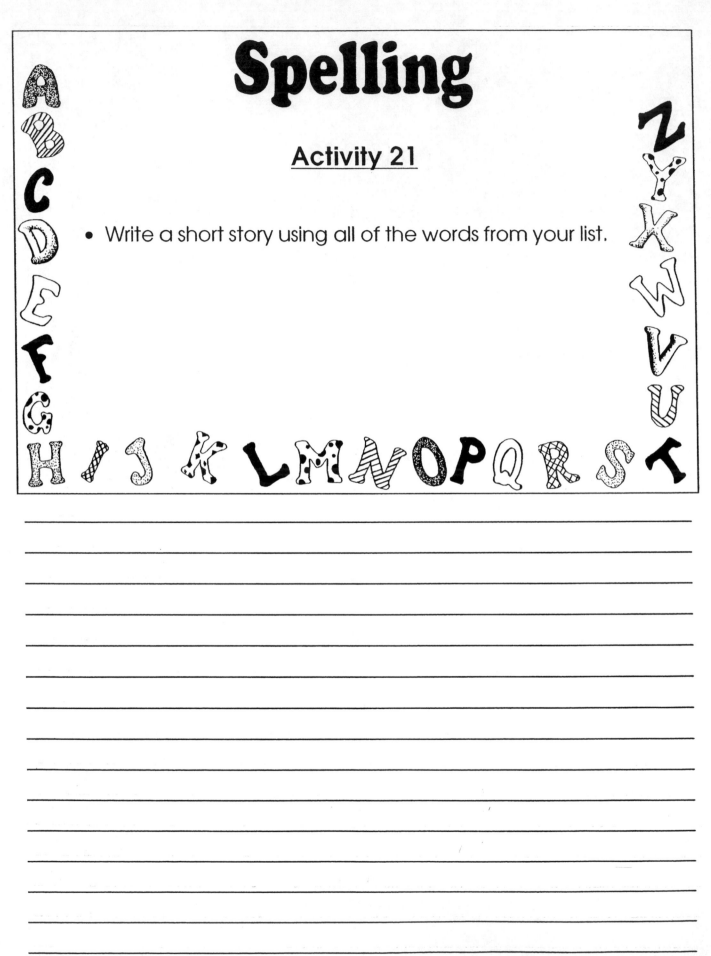

_____

_____

_____

_____

_____

_____

_____

_____

_____

_____

_____

_____

_____

Spelling

Activity 22

- Look at the words in your list.

- Write one complete sentence telling about the pattern you see.

_____

_____

_____

_____

_____

_____

_____

_____

_____

_____

_____

_____

_____

Spelling

Activity 23

- Use the letters in one of your spelling words to create a new word.

- Do this for every word in your list.

Example: dope - pod

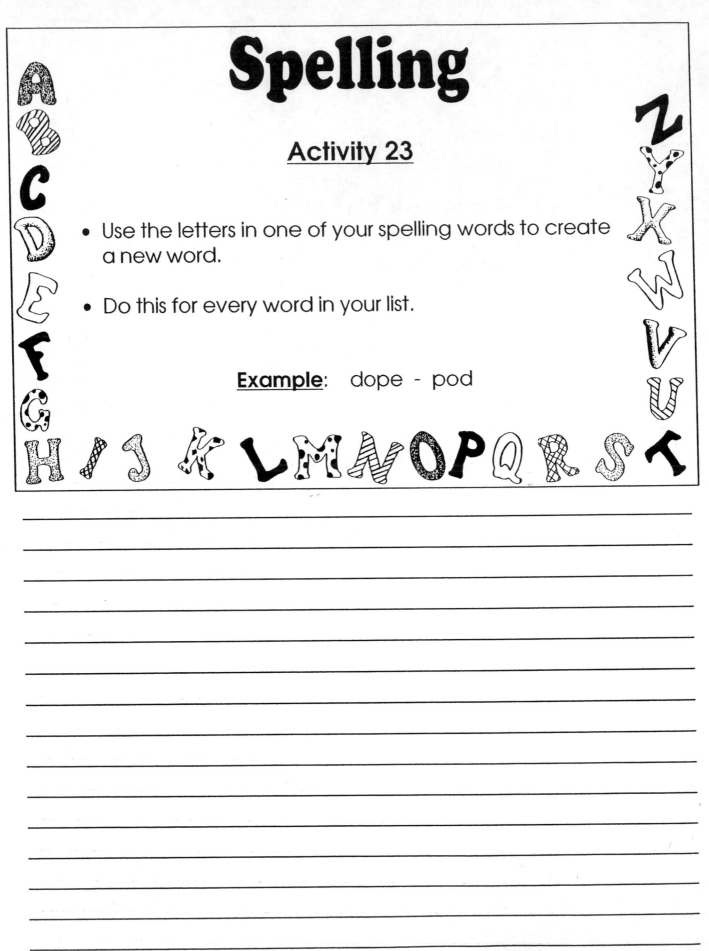

_____

_____

_____

_____

_____

_____

_____

_____

_____

_____

_____

_____

_____

Spelling

Activity 24

- Create an acrostic poem with a word from your list.

Example: **S**ilently

Neatly

Overpowering

White

Multi-Level Spelling

Spelling Lists

The title of each list indicates the skill for the week. The lists are in order of difficulty (List One is the easiest to List Five, the most difficult).

Blank sheets can be found at the back of this unit and are provided to allow you to create your own multi-level spelling lists if you find words your students need to practice but aren't found within these lists.

Short & Long oo/ough

List 1	List 2	List 3	List 4	List 5
book	shook	wooden	goodness	floo...
took	brook	goodbye	crooke...	
looks	stood	bloody		
poor	broom			
too	tooth			
noon	spoon			
tools	foolish			
fool	proof			
tough	enough			
rough	tougher			

Long a (ai, ay, a-e)

List 1	List 2	List 3	List 4	List 5
wait	afraid	sustain	restrain	quaint
rainy	remain	complain	proclaim	acquaintances
plane	saint	again	complaint	compaign
wave	again	waist	exclaim	straight
always	flake	waste	erase	fabricate
gray	plate	disgrace	demonstrate	eliminate
pay	taste	locate	indicate	estimate
brave	pathway	holiday	evade	dedicate
trade	sway	yesterday	portray	delayed
play	tray	highway	Tuesday	Saturday

Short a

List 1	List 2	List 3	List 4	List 5
camp	half	afternoon	wrap	anticipate
bath	cabin	began	appear	fashion
back	jacket	tackle	cheetah	appointed
clap	thank	manners	detach	transient
glad	above	camel	transport	astonishment
ask	stamp	cramp	transit	accomplish
damp	flash	blast	accept	sympathetic
crab	grant	master	manual	transaction
flat	baskets	mammal	January	adjective
mast	gallop	calves	ambulance	captivating

Short e

List 1	List 2	List 3	List 4	List 5
end	better	else	welcome	assignment
left	enjoy	basket	sweater	agency
help	tenth	angel	leather	college
send	women	elephant	feather	objectives
belt	pencil	happen	weather	prescription
fence	whenever	hundred	example	estimate
sell	whatever	twelve	inventor	celebrate
shell	myself	twenty	debt	effective
next	gravel	everywhere	prevent	chemistry
yet	shovel	travel	event	accept

Short i

List 1	List 2	List 3	List 4	List 5
swim	finger	admit	inflate	admittance
dim	written	submit	disagree	persistence
grim	wrist	display	positive	optometrist
little	quick	whistle	important	dictionary
wind	twinkle	whiskers	unicorn	transcontinental
pick	unit	whisper	gingerbread	humidifier
illness	until	impact	gymnastics	antiseptic
ticket	instead	income	insurance	immigrated
witch	invite	exist	involved	authorities
which	finish	shimmer	image	responsibility

Short o

List 1	List 2	List 3	List 4	List 5
cannot	gallop	poplar	October	oxidation
chop	body	wonder	concern	operation
cotton	doctor	October	clockwise	obstinate
from	problem	another	convert	opposite
hopped	across	coffee	octagon	nocturnal
rocky	Monday	cotton	volume	component
soft	front	bottle	abolish	controversy
softly	forgot	toxic	consumer	optimism
frost	block	bronze	impossible	paradox
flock	lesson	method	riot	economy

Short u

List 1	List 2	List 3	List 4	List 5
until	ugly	August	products	deduction
uncle	number	hundred	difficult	structural
dust	much	understand	public	misunderstanding
summer	butter	butterfly	autumn	obstruction
Sunday	bathtub	jungle	column	submitted
upset	rusty	lunches	supply	uncooperative
lunch	study	plus	culture	triumph
much	unless	umbrella	husband	result
rust	unable	bunches	budget	upholster
bump	under	until	distrust	unpublished

9/2# (handwritten note above List 3)

Long a (ai, ay, a-e)

List 1	List 2	List 3	List 4	List 5
wait	afraid	sustain	restrain	quaint
rainy	remain	complain	proclaim	acquaintances
plane	saint	again	complaint	complain
wave	again	waist	exclaim	straight
always	flake	waste	erase	fabricate
gray	plate	disgrace	demonstrate	eliminate
pay	taste	locate	indicate	estimate
brave	pathway	holiday	evade	dedicate
trade	sway	yesterday	portray	delayed
play	tray	highway	Tuesday	Saturday

10-1

Long e (ee, ea, e-e)

List 1	List 2	List 3	List 4	List 5
seem	street	speech	esteem	agreement
feel	freeze	between	referee	employees
peel	cheering	pioneer	employee	referee
feed	teeth	screech	underneath	pedigree
seen	speech	disagree	beneath	realization
been	east	eastern	realize	creativity
each	treat	dreary	reality	wreath
read	plead	treason	league	league
please	teacher	season	incomplete	obsolete
clean	reason	greasy	stampede	incomplete

10-9

Long i (ie, igh, i-e)

List 1	List 2	List 3	List 4	List 5
ride	tribe	quite	profile	paradise
lime	alike	empire	porcupine	merchandise
fine	stripe	desire	sterile	retirement
bike	quite	despite	generalize	generalize
rise	mile	describe	missile	sympathize
size	strike	vampire	empire	deodorize
high	night	brighten	lighten	frightening
fight	tighten	copyright	twilight	delightfully
light	delight	lightning	midnight	foresight
die	tries	denied	justified	petrified

Long o (ow, oa, i-e, old)

List 1	List 2	List 3	List 4	List 5
vote	impose	ozone	wardrobe	episode
spoke	globe	bolted	telescope	oppose
float	coach	motorboat	motorboats	torpedo
roast	throat	gloat	oatmeal	threshold
own	shown	growth	overthrown	voltage
yellow	fellow	sorrow	shadowy	thunderbolt
mold	olden	scolding	disown	coaches
gold	colder	blindfold	threshold	cocoa
bold	retold	household	marigold	shadowy
colt	molt	revolt	voltage	abroad

Long u

List 1	List 2	List 3	List 4	List 5
June	huge	computer	truthful	astute
tube	fluke	consume	parachute	constitute
rule	cute	dilute	introduce	ridicule
dune	cube	excuse	reduce	accumulated
huge	flute	refuse	produce	immunity
rude	fuse	include	persecute	revenue
fume	yule	amuse	execute	introducing
abuse	refuse	volume	manual	persecution
cute	excuse	reuse	salute	overpopulation
cube	human	useless	union	confusion

R-Controlled Vowels (er, ir, ur)

List 1	List 2	List 3	List 4	List 5
river	order	another	servant	property
ever	teacher	every	lantern	interesting
under	eraser	camera	whatever	handkerchief
paper	serve	evergreen	energy	universal
third	twirl	thirty	confirm	circulatory
squirt	birthday	swirl	thirsty	dirtier
girl	first	squirm	squirt	required
Saturday	Saturday	turtle	squirming	nocturnal
hurt	churn	furnish	occur	manufacturing
turn	burst	turkey	furnishing	enduring

R-Controlled Vowels (ar, or)

List 1	List 2	List 3	List 4	List 5
chart	alarm	marble	depart	sarcastic
hard	garden	carpenter	garland	article
harm	artist	harmful	sharpener	compartment
sharp	harder	sharpen	department	argument
yard	pardon	cartoon	artistic	characteristics
for	store	razor	editor	director
form	north	visitor	favorite	introductory
work	report	normal	inventor	transforming
forgot	stories	tornado	victory	foreign
sport	organ	worth	factory	orchestra

ow/ou

List 1	List 2	List 3	List 4	List 5
town	brown	power	allowed	allowance
now	clown	flower	sunflower	cowardice
how	frown	towel	vowels	chowder
owl	growl	prowl	coward	endow
howl	tower	growl	scowling	sunflower
out	south	mouth	crouch	mountaineer
ouch	hound	trout	aloud	profound
loud	cloudy	crouch	proudest	devout
round	couch	grouchy	cloudier	recount
pout	ground	bound	fountain	accounting

oi/oy

List 1	List 2	List 3	List 4	List 5
oil	broil	tinfoil	poison	poisonous
join	spoil	uncoil	devoid	asteroids
coin	joining	void	rejoice	turquoise
point	choice	avoiding	moist	avoided
boil	moist	rejoin	spoiling	embroidery
boy	enjoys	enjoying	disappoint	turmoil
joy	decoy	employ	employee	annoyance
cowboy	overjoy	convoy	loyalty	unemployment
toys	royal	destroy	royalty	employer
enjoy	overjoy	voyage	enjoyable	disappointed

ung, ing, ong, ung

List 1	List 2	List 3	List 4	List 5
bang	clang	sprang	boomerang	kangaroo
hang	tangy	mustang	kangaroo	boomerang
sang	hanging	twang	mustangs	mustangs
ring	spring	coloring	considering	terminating
king	finding	string	according	apologizing
sting	morning	finger	bilingual	strongest
long	along	prong	strongly	wrong
song	gong	belong	among	belongings
clung	slung	strung	oblong	prolonging
hung	swung	sprung	jungle	bungalow

Short & Long oo/ough

List 1	List 2	List 3	List 4	List 5
book	shook	wooden	goodness	floodlight
took	brook	goodbye	crooked	bloodhound
looks	stood	bloody	overlook	understood
poor	broom	school	moody	bassoon
too	tooth	goose	tycoon	gloominess
noon	spoon	snoop	swooning	schooner
tools	foolish	wooly	woolen	wooliest
fool	proof	doomed	snoopy	ought
tough	enough	through	throughout	thorough
rough	tougher	though	although	thoughtfulness

sh/ch/th

List 1	List 2	List 3	List 4	List 5
shut	shark	slash	shiny	shoulder
short	splash	shopping	sheriff	shellac
crush	crushing	finish	refreshing	shuffling
chips	charm	chopping	drenched	enchanting
child	chest	children	chapter	champion
much	chant	branch	clenched	chocolate
than	thing	these	northern	athlete
think	thinking	thrash	pathway	theatre
thank	thanking	cloth	clothes	thoughtlessly
thing	these	through	thought	thoughtful

wh/ph/hard and soft ch

List 1	List 2	List 3	List 4	List 5
who	what	what's	whisper	whichever
what	which	whenever	whether	wheelbarrow
when	whack	wheeze	wheelchair	whispering
why	whale	which	whistle	whistling
whiff	wheat	telephone	photocopy	photograph
phone	phase	elephant	nephew	physician
photo	phony	ache	stomach	orchestra
echo	echo	Christmas	character	chameleon
chord	chords	choirs	schedule	chemistry
chef	chefs	chute	charades	chauffeur

r-Blends

List 1	List 2	List 3	List 4	List 5
brand	broke	brushes	brief	breathe
cramp	branch	broad	broad	bronchitis
drown	draw	dressing	dread	dreadfulness
drop	dressed	driving	dreamy	drawbridge
free	fresh	French	freight	freighter
frog	Friday	fright	frighten	frighteningly
grand	great	greatest	grief	groceries
print	pretty	prize	proof	productive
tree	trick	trade	traffic	transportation
try	tried	trout	transport	traveling

s-Blends

List 1	List 2	List 3	List 4	List 5
scar	scare	scout	scarf	scissors
skip	skipped	skipping	skeleton	skeletal
sled	sleep	sleepy	slippery	slightly
small	smallest	smiling	smudge	smoulder
snail	snowing	snapped	sneaking	snowmobile
spill	spilled	spending	spoiled	special
spot	spotted	spoil	speaker	splendid
stop	stopping	stayed	strangely	steadily
stiff	stage	strange	standard	stationary
swim	swimming	sweeping	switch	switching

l-Blends

List 1	List 2	List 3	List 4	List 5
blind	blinded	blaze	bluffing	bleary
block	blocked	blindly	blackboard	blizzard
class	classes	climb	clothes	clearance
clown	clear	closing	claim	clutching
flag	flower	floated	flavor	flavorful
flat	flock	flying	flounder	flourishing
glad	glove	glasses	glanced	glorious
plan	plain	pleased	pleasant	pleasantly
plane	played	plenty	pleasure	pleasurable
slip	slippery	sliding	slight	slightly

Triple Blends

List 1	List 2	List 3	List 4	List 5
scrap	scrape	scribble	scrambled	scratchy
scrub	scroll	scratch	screaming	scrumptious
squat	squint	square	squashed	squeezable
shred	shrink	shredding	shrivel	shrubbery
spray	sprang	springing	sprinkle	sprinkler
spring	spraying	sprouted	spruce	sprawling
strong	stringy	strange	streaming	strenghthening
straw	strike	straight	stretched	strategies
three	threw	thread	through	throughout
thrash	thrashing	throat	threaten	threatening

Contractions

List 1	List 2	List 3	List 4	List 5
it's	haven't	didn't	shouldn't	where's
don't	we're	doesn't	wouldn't	shouldn't
I'll	what's	how's	doesn't	they've
I'm	he's	wasn't	won't	aren't
isn't	who's	we'll	they're	you're
he'll	she'll	you'd	who'll	they'll
he'd	you've	we've	they'd	we're
can't	we'd	she'd	won't	doesn't
she's	didn't	you're	you'll	its
I've	let's	they'll	couldn't	it's

Compound Words

List 1	List 2	List 3	List 4	List 5
inside	sometime	sunshine	newspaper	runaway
maybe	whenever	postman	daybreak	landlord
forget	forgot	someone	pineapple	cupboard
football	anyone	anyhow	daylight	screwdriver
anyhow	understand	butterfly	pincushion	warehouse
whoever	everywhere	sunrise	boxcars	clockwise
anything	baseball	somebody	hailstones	leadership
nobody	anywhere	buttermilk	pancakes	wherever
without	afternoon	doghouse	policeman	butterscotch
yourself	snowman	raindrops	wherever	watermelon
somehow	outside	airplanes	manpower	policemen

Homonyms

List 1	List 2	List 3	List 4	List 5
too	know	heard	their	piece
two	no	herd	there	peace
to	blue	you	they're	principal
sale	blew	ewe	you	principle
sail	one	marry	you're	guest
meat	won	merry	close	guessed
meet	sun	berry	clothes	way
by	son	bury	we're	weight
buy	knew	right	where	rain
bye	new	write	wear	reign

Silent Letters

List 1	List 2	List 3	List 4	List 5
lamb	watch	talking	walked	calmly
comb	wrap	doubt	calming	knowledge
palm	catch	calmly	wrinkly	knowledgeable
know	knitting	wrinkle	gnaw	gnarled
kneel	thumb	wrecked	knuckles	gnome
wrong	wrist	knew	doubtful	wrath
said	calm	debt	wrestling	rhinoceros
write	knowing	knock	knocked	colonel
wreck	knot	numb	knowingly	tongue
knob	wring	rhyme	design	campaign

Prefixes: ir/im/em/il/in

Please remember that some of these words do not contain "true" prefixes but rather are words that begin with the same letter combinations. You might want to point this out to your students.

List 1

iron
embed
impact
implant
illtimed
input
index
indoor
inside
inner

List 2

irate
embedded
imperfect
import
illfated
income
inform
insect
insert
intend

List 3

irritate
empower
improve
impulse
illegal
interest
interview
intercept
invite
involve

List 4

irregular
embraced
impossible
improvement
illustrate
interesting
invisible
incapable
invitation
insulting

List 5

irrational
emphasize
immaculate
impression
illegitimate
inexpensive
inexperienced
ineffective
international
insurance

Prefixes: re/dis/un/be

Please remember that some of these words do not contain "true" prefixes but rather are words that begin with the same letter combinations. You might want to point this out to your students.

List 1	List 2	List 3	List 4	List 5
reread	remain	rewritten	remember	recommend
replay	rebuild	refrain	redecorate	reproduction
retake	rewrite	recharge	reconsider	reschedule
dislike	dispose	distance	disconnect	disappointed
display	disrupt	disgrace	disappear	discouraged
dismiss	dismissed	dismissing	discontinue	discriminate
unfit	unable	unspent	undercover	uncertain
until	unarmed	unchained	unfriendly	unexceptional
become	beware	becoming	believe	behaviour
before	became	between	behalf	beneath

Prefixes: de/fore/post/ex

Please remember that some of these words do not contain "true" prefixes but rather are words that begin with the same letter combinations. You might want to point this out to your students.

List 1	List 2	List 3	List 4	List 5
defend	destroy	detour	departed	dejected
degree	delay	dethrone	deflated	delightfully
depart	defrost	debrief	decade	delivery
defog	decode	derailed	decrease	designing
dear	desert	deliver	defending	desirable
foreman	foreword	forefinger	forewarned	foreign
forehead	forecast	forewarn	foreshadow	foreclosure
post	postpone	postmarked	postponing	postgraduate
exit	excite	excuse	exchange	exhibition
extra	expert	expense	exclaim	extensively

Prefixes: uni/mono/bi/tri

Please remember that some of these words do not contain "true" prefixes but rather are words that begin with the same letter combinations. You might want to point this out to your students.

List 1	List 2	List 3	List 4	List 5
unit	unicorn	union	universe	university
unite	unicycle	united	unison	unidirectional
monorail	monocle	monograph	monotonous	monochromatic
monotone	monogram	monograms	monopoly	monolingual
biplane	biweekly	biceps	biology	biography
bikini	bicycle	bicycling	binoculars	biodegradable
trio	triplets	triangle	trivial	triplicate
triple	tripod	triceps	triangular	triceratops

Prefixes: sub/super/ultra/over/auto/mid

Please remember that some of these words do not contain "true" prefixes but rather are words that begin with the same letter combinations. You might want to point this out to your students.

List 1	List 2	List 3	List 4	List 5
subway	subject	submerge	submarine	subordinate
submit	subtract	subscribe	substitute	substantial
superb	superpower	superhuman	supervise	superintendent
superman	supermarket	supersonic	superior	superstitious
ultrafit	ultrasound	ultrasonic	ultraviolet	ultraviolet
overall	overdue	overhand	overseas	overanxious
overtime	overheat	overflowing	overshadow	oversensitive
autopilot	automatic	automobile	autograph	autobiography
midair	middle	midsummer	midyear	midstream
midway	midday	midnight	midwinter	midst

Prefixes: semi/trans/anti/mis/mal

Please remember that some of these words do not contain "true" prefixes but rather are words that begin with the same letter combinations. You might want to point this out to your students.

List 1	List 2	List 3	List 4	List 5
semidry	semipublic	semicircle	semiannual	semiautomatic
semifinal	semisoft	semisweet	semiskilled	semiconscious
transfer	transmit	transmitter	transparent	transcontinental
transit	transplant	transport	transmission	transformation
antic	antibody	antiseptic	antimagnetic	antiperspirant
antifreeze	antidote	antique	antibiotic	antisocial
misfit	misread	mistrust	mislabel	misunderstanding
mishap	misuse	misspell	mistaken	misbehaving
mallet	maltreat	maltreated	maladjusted	malnourished
male	malformed	malformed	malfunction	malnutrition

Suffixes: ick/ic

List 1	List 2	List 3	List 4	List 5
sick	trick	tricky	quickly	quicksand
tick	brick	sticking	tickle	flickering
topic	basic	music	musical	magnetic
comic	public	dramatic	tragic	microscopic
attic	metric	traffic	magical	gigantic
toxic	mimic	electric	gigantic	electronic
picnic	antics	elastic	artistic	arithmetic
basic	frantic	romantic	fantastic	statistics
panic	plastic	magnetic	historic	majestic
relic	comics	hectic	athletic	characteristics

Suffixes: ly/le

List 1	List 2	List 3	List 4	List 5
softly	slowly	really	quietly	usually
silly	lovely	happily	importantly	responsibly
sadly	loudly	finally	probably	considerably
only	simply	properly	beautifully	continually
costly	orderly	ability	exactly	permanently
little	cycle	people	article	available
beetle	uncle	circle	example	probable
paddle	cattle	marble	tremble	valuable
candle	handle	tumble	capable	reasonable
apple	fiddle	stable	assemble	responsible

Suffixes: less/ness/ful/ship/hood

List 1	List 2	List 3	List 4	List 5
shoeless	hopeless	careless	thankless	heartless
sickness	fitness	blackness	brightness	truthfulness
illness	darkness	greatness	swiftness	thoughtlessness
kindness	dampness	strictness	suddenness	naturalness
gladness	newness	rudeness	strangeness	gloominess
joyful	skillful	healthful	beautiful	resourceful
hopeful	thankful	truthful	dreadful	frightful
kinship	friendship	courtship	relationship	championship
manhood	brotherhood	falsehood	adulthood	neighborhood
childhood	sisterhood	likelihood	livelihood	womanhood

Suffixes: ent/able/ible/al

List 1	List 2	List 3	List 4	List 5
sent	spent	prevents	retirement	advertisement
parent	event	present	president	accident
bent	basement	statement	management	requirement
went	agreement	transparent	equipment	government
lent	prevent	experiment	disappointment	parliament
table	stable	disable	adorable	unavoidable
cable	usable	passable	removable	detachable
likable	readable	unstable	vegetable	indispensable
flexible	horrible	responsible	convertible	digestible
dial	general	material	industrial	educational
vial	trial	special	national	chemical

Suffixes. tion/sion/ive/ity

List 1	List 2	List 3	List 4	List 5
nation	emotion	inflation	medication	presentation
lotion	devotion	nutrition	ignition	jubilation
potion	donation	fashion	imitation	identification
station	nation	estimation	recognition	premonition
ration	vacation	position	calculation	organization
motion	condition	rotation	publication	impersonation
active	reactive	creative	productive	impressive
motive	reality	community	maturity	responsibility
oddity	ability	captivity	university	objectivity

Multi-Level Spelling

Spelling

_____

_____

_____

_____

_____

_____

_____

_____

_____

_____

_____

_____

_____

_____

_____

Publication Listing

See Dealer or www.onthemarkpress.com For Pricing 1-800-463-6367

Code #	Title and Grade
OTM-1492	Abel's Island NS 4-6
OTM-1131	Addition & Subtraction Drills Gr. 1-3
OTM-1128	Addition Drills Gr. 1-3
OTM-2504	Addition Gr. 1-3
OTM-14174	Adv. of Huckle Berry Finn NS 7-8
OTM-293	All About Dinosaurs Gr. 2
OTM-102	All About Mexico Gr. 4-6
OTM-120	All About the Ocean Gr. 5-7
OTM-249	All About the Sea Gr. 4-6
OTM-261	All About Weather Gr. 7-8
OTM-2110	All Kinds of Structures Gr. 1
OTM-601	Amazing Aztecs Gr. 4-6
OTM-1468	Amelia Bedelia NS 1-3
OTM-113	America The Beautiful Gr. 4-6
OTM-1457	Amish Adventure NS 7-8
OTM-602	Ancient China Gr. 4-6
OTM-618	Ancient Egypt Gr. 4-6
OTM-621	Ancient Greece Gr. 4-6
OTM-619	Ancient Rome Gr. 4-6
OTM-1453	Anne of Green Gables NS 7-8
OTM-14162	Arnold Lobel Author Study Gr. 2-3
OTM-1622	Australia B/W Pictures
OTM-105	Australia Gr. 5-8
OTM-14224	Banner in the Sky NS 7-8
OTM-401	Be Safe Not Sorry Gr. P-1
OTM-1409	Bear Tales Gr. 2-4
OTM-14202	Bears in Literature Gr. 1-3
OTM-1440	Beatrix Potter Gr. 2-4
OTM-14129	Beatrix Potter: Activity Biography Gr. 2-4
OTM-14257	Because of Winn-Dixie NS Gr. 4-6
OTM-14114	Best Christmas Pageant Ever NS Gr. 4-6
OTM-14107	Borrowers NS Gr. 4-6
OTM-1463	Bridge to Terabithia NS Gr. 4-6
OTM-2524	BTS Numeración Gr. 1-3
OTM-2525	BTS Adición Gr. 1-3
OTM-2526	BTS Sustracción Gr. 1-3
OTM-2527	BTS Fonética Gr. 1-3
OTM-2528	BTS Leer para Entender Gr. 1-3
OTM-2529	BTS Uso de las Mayúsculas y Reglas de Puntuación Gr. 1-3
OTM-2530	BTS Composición de Oraciones Gr. 1-3
OTM-2531	BTS Composici13n de Historias Gr. 1-3
OTM-14256	Bud, Not Buddy NS Gr. 4-6
OTM-1807	Building Word Families L.V. 1-2
OTM-1805	Building Word Families S.V. 1-2
OTM-14164	Call It Courage NS Gr. 7-8
OTM-1467	Call of the Wild NS Gr. 7-8
OTM-2507	Capitalization & Punctuation Gr. 1-3
OTM-14198	Captain Courageous NS Gr. 7-8
OTM-14154	Castle in the Attic NS Gr. 4-6
OTM-631	Castles & Kings Gr. 4-6
OTM-1434	Cats in Literature Gr. 3-6
OTM-14212	Cay NS Gr. 7-8
OTM-2107	Cells, Tissues & Organs Gr. 7-8
OTM-2101	Characteristics of Flight Gr. 4-6
OTM-1466	Charlie and Chocolate Factory NS Gr. 4-6
OTM-1423	Charlotte's Web NS Gr. 4-6
OTM-109	China Today Gr. 5-8
OTM-1470	Chocolate Fever NS Gr. 4-6
OTM-14241	Chocolate Touch NS Gr. 4-6
OTM-14104	Classical Poetry Gr. 7-12
OTM-811	Community Helpers Gr. 1-3
OTM-14183	Copper Sunrise NS Gr. 7-8
OTM-1486	Corduroy and Pocket Corduroy NS Gr. 1-3
OTM-234	Creatures of the Sea Gr. 2-4
OTM-14208	Curse of the Viking Grave NS 7-8
OTM-1121	Data Management Gr. 4-6
OTM-253	Dealing with Dinosaurs Gr. 4-6
OTM-14105	Dicken's Christmas NS Gr. 7-8
OTM-1621	Dinosaurs B/W Pictures
OTM-216	Dinosaurs Gr. 1
OTM-14175	Dinosaurs in Literature Gr. 1-3
OTM-2106	Diversity of Living Things Gr. 4-6
OTM-1127	Division Drills Gr. 4-6
OTM-287	Down by the Sea Gr. 1-3
OTM-1416	Dragons in Literature Gr. 3-6
OTM-2109	Earth's Crust Gr. 6-8
OTM-1612	Egypt B/W Pictures
OTM-14255	Egypt Game NS Gr. 4-6
OTM-628	Egyptians Today and Yesterday Gr. 2-3
OTM-2108	Electricity Gr. 4-6
OTM-285	Energy Gr. 4-6
OTM-2123	Environment Gr. 4-6
OTM-1812	ESL Teaching Ideas Gr. K-8
OTM-14258	Esperanza Rising NS Gr. 4-6
OTM-1822	Exercises in Grammar Gr. 6
OTM-1823	Exercises in Grammar Gr. 7
OTM-1824	Exercises in Grammar Gr. 8
OTM-620	Exploration Gr. 4-6
OTM-1054	Exploring Canada Gr. 1-3
OTM-1056	Exploring Canada Gr. 1-6
OTM-1055	Exploring Canada Gr. 4-6
OTM-820	Exploring My School and Community Gr. 1
OTM-1639	Fables B/W Pictures
OTM-1415	Fables Gr. 4-6
OTM-14168	First 100 Sight Words Gr. 1
OTM-14170	Flowers for Algernon NS Gr. 7-8
OTM-14128	Fly Away Home NS Gr. 4-6
OTM-405	Food: Fact, Fun & Fiction Gr. 1-3
OTM-406	Food: Nutrition & Invention Gr. 4-6
OTM-2118	Force and Motion Gr. 1-3
OTM-2119	Force and Motion Gr. 4-6
OTM-14172	Freckle Juice NS Gr. 1-3
OTM-14209	Giver, The NS Gr. 7-8
OTM-1114	Graph for all Seasons Gr. 1-3
OTM-1490	Great Expectations NS Gr. 7-8
OTM-14169	Great Gilly Hopkins NS Gr. 4-6
OTM-14238	Greek Mythology Gr. 7-8
OTM-2113	Growth & Change in Animals Gr. 2-3
OTM-2114	Growth & Change in Plants Gr. 2-3
OTM-2104	Habitats Gr. 4-6
OTM-14205	Harper Moon NS Gr. 7-8
OTM-14136	Hatchet NS Gr. 7-8
OTM-14184	Hobbit NS Gr. 7-8
OTM-14250	Holes NS Gr. 4-6
OTM-1848	How To Give a Presentation Gr. 4-6
OTM-14125	How To Teach Writing Through 7-9
OTM-1810	How To Write a Composition 6-10
OTM-1809	How To Write a Paragraph 5-10
OTM-1808	How To Write an Essay Gr. 7-12
OTM-1803	How To Write Poetry & Stories 4-6
OTM-407	Human Body Gr. 2-4
OTM-402	Human Body Gr. 4-6
OTM-605	In Days of Yore Gr. 4-6
OTM-606	In Pioneer Days Gr. 2-4
OTM-241	Incredible Dinosaurs Gr. P-1
OTM-14177	Incredible Journey NS Gr. 4-6
OTM-14100	Indian in the Cupboard NS Gr. 4-6
OTM-14193	Island of the Blue Dolphins NS 4-6
OTM-1465	James & The Giant Peach NS 4-6
OTM-1625	Japan B/W Pictures
OTM-106	Japan Gr. 5-8
OTM-1461	Julie of the Wolves NS Gr. 7-8
OTM-502	Junior Music for Fall Gr. 4-6
OTM-505	Junior Music for Spring Gr. 4-6
OTM-506	Junior Music Made Easy for Winter Gr. 4-6
OTM-14140	Kids at Bailey School Gr. 2-4
OTM-298	Learning About Dinosaurs Gr. 3
OTM-1122	Learning About Measurement Gr. 1-3
OTM-1119	Learning About Money USA Gr. 1-3
OTM-1123	Learning About Numbers Gr. 1-3
OTM-269	Learning About Rocks and Soils Gr. 2-3
OTM-1108	Learning About Shapes Gr. 1-3
OTM-2100	Learning About Simple Machines Gr. 1-3
OTM-1104	Learning About the Calendar Gr. 2-3
OTM-1110	Learning About Time Gr. 1-3
OTM-1450	Legends Gr. 4-6
OTM-14130	Life & Adv. of Santa Claus NS 7-8
OTM-210	Life in a Pond Gr. 3-4
OTM-630	Life in the Middle Ages Gr. 7-8
OTM-2103	Light & Sound Gr. 4-6
OTM-14219	Light in the Forest NS Gr. 7-8
OTM-1446	Lion, Witch & the Wardrobe NS 4-6
OTM-1851	Literature Response Forms Gr. 1-3
OTM-1852	Literature Response Forms Gr. 4-6
OTM-14233	Little House on the Prairie NS 4-6
OTM-14109	Lost in the Barrens NS Gr. 7-8
OTM-14167	Magic School Bus Gr. 1-3
OTM-14247	Magic Treehouse Gr. 1-3
OTM-278	Magnets Gr. 3-5
OTM-403	Making Sense of Our Senses K-1
OTM-294	Mammals Gr. 1
OTM-295	Mammals Gr. 2
OTM-296	Mammals Gr. 3
OTM-297	Mammals Gr. 5-6
OTM-14160	Maniac Magee NS Gr. 4-6
OTM-119	Mapping Activities & Outlines! 4-8
OTM-117	Mapping Skills Gr. 1-3
OTM-107	Mapping Skills Gr. 4-6
OTM-2116	Matter & Materials Gr. 1-3
OTM-2117	Matter & Materials Gr. 4-6
OTM-1609	Medieval Life B/W Pictures
OTM-1413	Mice in Literature Gr. 3-5
OTM-14180	Midnight Fox NS Gr. 4-6
OTM-1118	Money Talks – Gr. 3-6
OTM-1497	Mouse & the Motorcycle NS 4-6
OTM-1494	Mr. Poppers Penguins NS Gr. 4-6
OTM-14201	Mrs. Frisby & Rats NS Gr. 4-6
OTM-1826	Multi-Level Spelling USA Gr. 3-6
OTM-1132	Multiplication & Division Drills 4-6
OTM-1130	Multiplication Drills Gr. 4-6
OTM-114	My Country! The USA! Gr. 2-4
OTM-1437	Mystery at Blackrock Island NS 7-8
OTM-14157	Nate the Great and Sticky Case NS Gr. 1-3
OTM-110	New Zealand Gr. 4-8
OTM-1475	Novel Ideas Gr. 4-6
OTM-14244	Number the Stars NS Gr. 4-6
OTM-2503	Numeration Gr. 1-3
OTM-14220	One in Middle Green Kangaroo NS Gr. 1-3
OTM-272	Our Trash Gr. 2-3
OTM-2121	Our Universe Gr. 5-8
OTM-286	Outer Space Gr. 1-2
OTM-118	Outline Maps of the World Gr. 1-8
OTM-1431	Owls in the Family NS Gr. 4-6
OTM-1452	Paperbag Princess NS Gr. 1-3
OTM-212	Passport to Australia Gr. 4-5
OTM-1804	Personal Spelling Dictionary Gr. 2-5
OTM-503	Phantom of the Opera Gr. 6-9
OTM-14171	Phoebe Gilman Author Study Gr. 2-3
OTM-2506	Phonics Gr. 1-3
OTM-1448	Pigs in Literature Gr. 2-4
OTM-1499	Pinballs NS Gr. 4-6
OTM-634	Pirates Gr. 4-6
OTM-2120	Planets Gr. 3-6
OTM-1874	Poetry Prompts Gr. 1-3
OTM-1875	Poetry Prompts Gr. 4-6
OTM-624	Prehistoric Times Gr. 4-6
OTM-501	Primary Music for Fall Gr. 1-3
OTM-504	Primary Music for Spring Gr. 4-6
OTM-507	Primary Music Made Easy for Winter Gr. 1-3
OTM-1120	Probability & Inheritance Gr. 7-10
OTM-1426	Rabbits in Literature Gr. 2-4
OTM-1444	Ramona Quimby Age 8 NS 4-6
OTM-2508	Reading for Meaning Gr. 1-3
OTM-14234	Reading with Arthur Gr. 1-3
OTM-14200	Reading with Curious George 2-4
OTM-14230	Reading with Eric Carle Gr. 1-3
OTM-14251	Reading with Kenneth Oppel 4-6
OTM-1427	Reading with Mercer Mayer 1-2
OTM-14142	Reading with Robert Munsch 1-3
OTM-14225	River NS Gr. 7-8
OTM-508	Robert Schumann-Life & Times Gr. 6-9
OTM-265	Rocks & Minerals Gr. 4-6
OTM-14103	Sadako and 1 000 Paper Cranes NS Gr. 4-6
OTM-404	Safety Gr. 2-4
OTM-1442	Sarah Plain & Tall NS Gr. 4-6
OTM-1601	Sea Creatures B/W Pictures
OTM-279	Sea Creatures Gr. 1-3
OTM-1464	Secret Garden NS Gr. 4-6
OTM-2502	Sentence Writing Gr. 1-3
OTM-1430	Serendipity Series Gr. 3-5
OTM-1866	Shakespeare Shorts – Performing Arts Gr. 2-4
OTM-1867	Shakespeare Shorts – Performing Arts Gr. 4-6
OTM-1868	Shakespeare Shorts – Language Arts Gr. 2-4
OTM-1869	Shakespeare Shorts – Language Arts Gr. 4-6
OTM-14181	Sight Words Activities Gr. 1
OTM-299	Simple Machines Gr. 4-6
OTM-2122	Solar System Gr. 4-6
OTM-205	Space Gr. 2-3
OTM-1834	Spelling Blacklines Gr. 1
OTM-1835	Spelling Blacklines Gr. 2
OTM-1814	Spelling Gr. 1
OTM-1815	Spelling Gr. 2
OTM-1816	Spelling Gr. 3
OTM-1817	Spelling Gr. 4
OTM-1818	Spelling Gr. 5
OTM-1819	Spelling Gr. 6
OTM-1827	Spelling Worksavers #1 Gr. 3-5
OTM-2125	Stable Structures & Mechanisms 3
OTM-14139	Stone Fox NS Gr. 4-6
OTM-14214	Stone Orchard NS Gr. 7-8
OTM-1864	Story Starters Gr. 1-3
OTM-1865	Story Starters Gr. 4-6
OTM-1873	Story Starters Gr. 1-6
OTM-2509	Story Writing Gr. 1-3
OTM-2111	Structures, Mechanisms & Motion 2
OTM-14211	Stuart Little NS Gr. 4-6
OTM-1129	Subtraction Drills Gr. 1-3
OTM-2505	Subtraction Gr. 1-3
OTM-2511	Successful Language Pract. Gr. 1-3
OTM-2512	Successful Math Practice Gr. 1-3
OTM-2309	Summer Learning Gr. K-1
OTM-2310	Summer Learning Gr. 1-2
OTM-2311	Summer Learning Gr. 2-3
OTM-2312	Summer Learning Gr. 3-4
OTM-2313	Summer Learning Gr. 4-5
OTM-2314	Summer Learning Gr. 5-6
OTM-14159	Summer of the Swans NS Gr. 4-6
OTM-1418	Superfudge NS Gr. 4-6
OTM-108	Switzerland Gr. 4-6
OTM-115	Take a Trip to Australia Gr. 2-3
OTM-2102	Taking Off With Flight Gr. 1-3
OTM-1455	Tales of the Fourth Grade NS 4-6
OTM-1472	Ticket to Curlew NS Gr. 4-6
OTM-14222	To Kill a Mockingbird NS Gr. 7-8
OTM-14163	Traditional Poetry Gr. 7-10
OTM-1481	Tuck Everlasting NS Gr. 4-6
OTM-14126	Turtles in Literature Gr. 1-3
OTM-1427	Unicorns in Literature Gr. 3-5
OTM-617	Viking Age Gr. 4-6
OTM-14206	War with Grandpa NS Gr. 4-6
OTM-2124	Water Gr. 2-4
OTM-260	Weather Gr. 4-6
OTM-1417	Wee Folk in Literature Gr. 3-5
OTM-808	What is a Community? Gr. 2-4
OTM-262	What is the Weather Today? 2-4
OTM-1473	Where the Red Fern Grows NS 7-8
OTM-1487	Where the Wild Things Are NS 1-3
OTM-14187	Whipping Boy NS Gr. 4-6
OTM-14226	Who is Frances Rain? NS Gr. 4-6
OTM-509	Wolfgang Amadeus Mozart Gr. 6-9
OTM-14213	Wolf Island NS Gr. 1-3
OTM-14221	Wrinkle in Time NS Gr. 7-8